초등 **영어문장규칙** 배우기

# 기초문장·단어

# 따라쓰기

## 1

와이 앤 엠

# 차 례

초등 **영어문장규칙** 배우기

# 기초문장·단어
# 따라쓰기

## 1

## a. 명사

This is a table.
[ðis iz ə teibl]
이것은 테이블입니다

This is my bag.
[ðis iz mai bæg]
이것은 나의 가방입니다

That is a computer.
[ðæt iz ə kəmpiu:tər]
저것은 컴퓨터입니다

This is a table.  This is a table.

This is a table.  This is a table.

This is my bag. This is my bag.

This is my bag. This is my bag.

That is a computer.

That is a computer.

# 명사

## This is a bear.
[ðis iz ə ber]
이것은 곰입니다

## This is my banana.
[ðis iz mai bənænə]
이것은 나의 바나나입니다

## I am Sung-won
[ái æm səŋ-wʌ́n]
나는 성원입니다

This is a bear.　This is a bear.

This is a bear.　This is a bear.

This is my banana.　This is my banana.

This is my banana.　This is my banana.

I am Sung-won.　I am Sung-won.

I am Sung-won.　I am Sung-won.

사람 이름, 물건 이름, 동물 이름 등 모든 이름을 전부 명사라고
합니다. 그리고 명사는 다시 책이나 가방처럼 셀 수 있는 명사와
물이나 공기처럼 셀 수 없는 명사로 나뉩니다.

보기에서 골라 　　　　 속에 알맞은 명사를 쓰고 아래 따라 써 봅시다.

**❶ This is a**

이것은 곰이다.

This is a

---

**❷ This is  my**

이것은 테이블이다

This is my

**❸ That is a**

이것은 컴퓨터이다.

That is a

❹ This is my

이것은 나의 바나나이다.

This is my

❺ This is my

이것은 나의 가방이다.

This is my

❻ I am

나는 성원이다.

I am

단어를 따라 써 보세요

## bed
침대

[bed 뱃]

bed bed bed bed bed

## bell
종, 초인종

[bel 벨]

bell bell bell bell bell

## cap
모자

[kæp 캡]

cap cap cap cap

## chair
의자

[tʃɛər 췌어ㄹ]

chair chair chair chair chair

## coat
외투

[kout 코웃]

coat coat coat coat coat

## cup
컵

[kʌp 컵]

cup　cup　cup　cup　cup

## door
문

[dɔːr 도얼]

door　door　door　door

## family
가족

[fǽməli페믈리]

family　family　family　family

## garden
정원

[gáːrdn가-ㄹ든]

garden　garden　garden

## hand
손

[hænd 핸드]

hand　hand　hand　hand

## head
머리

[hed 헤드]

head　head　head　head

**home**

집

[hóum 홈]

home home home

---

**leg**

다리

[leg 렉]

leg leg leg leg

---

**mouth**

입

[mauθ 마웃쓰]

mouth mouth mouth mouth

---

**pants**

바지

[pænts 팬츠]

pants pants pants pants

---

**roof**

지붕

[ruːf 루-프]

roof roof roof roof roof

---

**room**

방

[ruːm 루-움]

room room room room

**shirt**

셔츠

[ʃəːrt 셔-ㄹ츠]

shirt　　shirt　　shirt　　shirt

**shoe**

신, 구두

[ʃuː 슈-]

shoe　　shoe　　shoe

**skirt**

스커트

[skəːrt 스꺼얼트]

skirt　　skirt　　skirt　　skirt

**sofa**

소파

[sóufə 쏘우풔]

sofa　　sofa　　sofa

**stair**

계단

[stɛər 스떼어]

stair　　stair　　stair　　stair

**son**

아들

[sɔn 썬]

son　son　son　son　son　son

# This is a doll.
[ðis iz ə dɑːl]

이것은 인형입니다

# I am a girl.
[ái æm ə gɜːrl]

나는 소녀입니다

# That is a crayon.
[ðæt iz ə kreiən]

저것은 크레용입니다

This is a doll    This is a doll

This is a doll    This is a doll

I am a girl.    I am a girl.

I am a girl.    I am a girl.

That is a crayon. That is a crayon.

That is a crayon. That is a crayon.

대명사는 명사를 대신하여 쓰이는 말로, 한글에서의 '나,너,우리,
이것,저것'에 해당하는 단어가 모두 그에 속합니다.

# 대명사

## We are friends.
[wi ə frenz]
우리는 친구입니다

## He is a teacher.
[hiːi iz ə tiːtʃər]
그는 선생님입니다

## This is a chair.
[ðis iz ə tʃer]
이것은 의자입니다

We are fiends.　　We are fiends.

We are fiends.　　We are fiends.

He is a teacher.　He is a teacher.

He is a teacher.　He is a teacher.

This is a chair.　　This is a chair.

This is a chair.　　This is a chair.

대명사는 다시, 1.인칭대명사(나,너,그,그녀와 같이 사람을 가리키는 대명사) 2.지시대명사(이것,이사람,저것,저사람처럼 사물을 대신하여 사용할 수 있는 대명사) 3.의문대명사(누가,왜,어떻게 등 무엇을 물을 때 사용하는 대명사) 4.부정대명사(모든,약간 등 정해져 있지 않은 사람이나 사물을 가리킬 때 사용하는 대명사)가 있습니다.

**❶** [          ] is a crayon.

저것은 크레용이다

_____

is a crayon.

**❷** [          ] am a girl.

나는 소녀이다

_____

am a girl.

**❸** [          ] are friends.

우리는 친구이다

_____

are friends.

18

This   That   We   I   He

❹ _____ is a teacher.

그는 선생님이다

_____

is a teacher.

❺ _____ is a doll.

이것은인형이다

_____

is a doll.

❻ _____ is a chair.

이것은 의자이다

_____

is a chair.

## 단어를 따라 써 보세요

### I
나는, 내가

[ai 아이]

I I I I I I I I I I

### my
나의

[maí 마이]

my my my my my my

### me
나를

[mi 미-]

me me me me me

### you
너, 당신

[ju: 유-]

you you you you

### your
너의, 너희들의

[juər 유얼]

your your your your your

| **he** | he he he he he he he |
| :---: | :--- |
| 그는, 그가 | |
| [hi: 히-] | |

| **his** | his his his his his |
| :---: | :--- |
| 그의, 그의 것 | |
| [híz 히이스] | |

| **him** | him him him him him |
| :---: | :--- |
| 그를, 그에게 | |
| [him 힘] | |

| **she** | she she she she |
| :---: | :--- |
| 그녀는, 그녀가 | |
| [ʃiː 쉬] | |

| **her** | her her her her her |
| :---: | :--- |
| 그녀의 | |
| [hə:r 허얼] | |

| **it** | it it it it it it it it it |
| :---: | :--- |
| 그것은 | |
| [it 잇] | |

## its
그것의

[its 잇즈]

its its its its its its its

## they
그들은

[ðei 데이]

they they they they

## them
그들을

[ðem 뎀]

them them them them

## we
우리, 저희가

[wiː 위-]

we we we we we

## our
우리의

[auər 아우월]

our our our our our

## us
우리들을

[ʌs 어쓰]

us us us us us us us

## this
이것

[ðis 디쓰]

this   this   this   this

## these
이것들

[ðíːz 디-즈]

these   these   these   these

## that
저것, 그것

[ðæt 댓]

that   that   that

## the
그

[ðə/ði 더/디]

the   the   the   the

## there
거기에

[ðɛər 데얼]

there   there   there   there

# C. 동사

## This is a chair.
[ðis iz ə tʃer]
이것은 의자입니다

## I am a boy.
[ái æm ə bɔi]
나는 소년입니다

## That is a dish.
[ðæt iz ə diʃ]
저것은 접시입니다

This is a chair   This is a chair

This is a chair   This is a chair

I am a boy. I am a boy. I am a boy.

I am a boy. I am a boy. I am a boy.

That is a dish.   That is a dish.

That is a dish.   That is a dish.

동사는 사람이나 사물의  움직임과, 한글에서의 '이다,~이 있다' 등를 나타내는 말입니다.

## You are beautiful.
[iə ər biu:tifl]

당신은 아름답습니다

## We go to shool.
[wi gou tu: sku:l]

우리는 학교에 갑니다

## She plays the piano.
[ʃi pleis ðə piænou]

그는 피아노를 칩니다

26

You are beautiful. You are beautiful.

You are beautiful. You are beautiful.

We go to school. We go to school.

We go to school. We go to school.

She plays the piano. She plays the piano.

She plays the piano. She plays the piano.

동사에는 1.일반동사 (사람이나 사물의 움직임을 나타내는 동사)와 2. Be 동사(~이다.와 ~이 있다의 뜻을 가진 동사) 3.조동사(동사의 뜻을 분명하게 해 주는 동사)가 있으며, 조동사 뒤에는 동사의 원형이 반드시 옵니다.

★ 보기에서 골라 [ ] 속에 알맞은 동사를 쓰고 아래 따라 써 봅시다.

**❶** I [ ] a boy.

나는 소년이다

I ___ a boy.

**❷** We [ ] to school.

우리는 학교에 간다

We ___ to shool.

**❸** She [ ] the piano

그는 피아노친다

She ___ the piano.

| 보기 | go | is | am | play | are |

❹ You      beautiful.

당신은 아름답다

You      beautiful.

❺ That      a dish.

저것은 접시이다

That      a dish.

❻ This      a chair.

이것은 의자이다

This      a chair.

단어를 따라 써 보세요

## burn
타다, 태우다

[bəːrn 버-ㄹ언]

burn    burn    burn    burn

## call
부르다

[kɔːl 커얼]

call    call    call    call    call

## carry
운반하다

[kǽri 캐뤼]

carry    carry    carry    carry

## catch
잡다, 받다

[kætʃ 캣취]

catch    catch    catch

## count
수를 세다

[kaunt 카운트]

count    count    count    count

**drink**
마시다
[driŋk 쥬륑크]

drink    drink    drink    drink

**drive**
운전하다
[draiv 드롸이브]

drive    drive    drive    drive

**enjoy**
즐기다
[éndʒɔ́i 엔줘이]

enjoy    enjoy    enjoy    enjoy

**find**
찾다, 발견하다
[faind 퐈인드]

find    find    find    find    find

**have**
가지고 있다
[hæv 해브]

have    have    have

**hold**
잡다, 붙들다
[hould 호울드]

hold    hold    hold    hold

**hurry**

서두르다

[həːri 허-뤼]

hurry hurry hurry hurry

**jump**

뛰어오르다

[dʒʌmp 점프]

jump jump jump

**keep**

계속하다

[kiːp 키-입]

keep keep keep keep

**kick**

차다

[kik 킥]

kick kick kick kick

**love**

사랑하다

[lɔv 러브]

love love love love

**meet**

만나다

[miːt 미잇트]

meet meet meet meet

**pass**

지나가다

[pæs 패스]

pass pass pass pass

**play**

연주하다, 놀다

[plei 플레이]

play play play

**ran**

달렸다

[ræn 뢘]

ran ran ran ran ran

**ride**

타다

[raid 롸이드]

ride ride ride ride

**see**

보다

[siː 씨-]

see see see see

**show**

보이다

[ʃou 쇼우]

show show show show

## He is smart.
[hiː iz smɑːrt]
그는 똑똑하다

## We are happy.
[wi ər hæpi]
우리는 행복하다

## He is a young boy.
[hiː iz ə iʌŋ bɔi]
그는 어린 소년이다

He is smart.　　He is smart.

He is smart.　　He is smart.

We are happy.　We are happy.

We are happy.　We are happy.

He is a young boy.　He is a young boy.

He is a young boy.　He is a young boy.

형용사는 모양이나 형상을 나타내는 말로, 주로 명사 앞에서 명사를 더 자세히 설명해 주며, be 동사와 함께 쓰입니다.

## She is beautiful.
[ʃi iz biuːtifl]
그녀는 아름답다

## We are smart.
[wi ər smaːrt]
우리는 똑똑하다

## He is ugly.
[hiː iz ʌgli]
그는 못생겼다

She is beautiful.  She is beautiful.

She is beautiful.  She is beautiful.

We are smart.   We are smart.

We are smart.   We are smart.

He is ugly.     He is ugly.

He is ugly.     He is ugly.

형용사에는 사람이나 사물의 많고 적음을 나타내는 형용사가 있는데 이를 수량형용사라고합니다.
 예를 들면 many(많은), a few(약간), few(거의 없는), much(많은), a little(약간),  little(거의 없는) 등과 같습니다.

★ 보기에서 골라 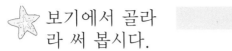 속에 알맞은 형용사를 쓰고 아래 따라 써 봅시다.

❶ He is

그는 똑똑하다

He is

❷ He is a ____ boy.

그는 어린 소년이다

He is a        boy.

❸ We are

우리는 행복하다

We are

smart  happy  young  beautiful ugly

**❹** She is

그녀는 아름답다

She is

**❺** He is

그는 못생겼다.

He is

**❻** We are

우리는 똑똑하다.

We are

**단어를 따라 써 보세요**

## angry
화난

[ǽŋgri 앵그뤼]

angry    angry    angry    angry

## any
무엇이든

[éni 애니]

any    any    any    any    any

## beautiful
아름다운

[bjúːtəfəl 뷰-러플]

beautiful    beautiful

yes

## close
가까운, 친한

[klous클로우즈]

close    close    close    close

## dead
죽은

[ded 데드]

dead    dead    dead    dead

## enough
충분한

[inʌ́f 이너프]

enough    enough    enough

## every
모든

[évri: 에브뤼]

every   every   every   every

## free
자유로운

[fri: 프뤼-]

free  free  free  free  free

## full
가득한, 충만한

[ful 풀]

full  full  full  full

## good
좋은, 착한

[gud 굿]

good    good    good

## hard
딱딱한, 어려운

[haːrd 하알드]

hard   hard   hard   hard

**hungry**
배고픈
[hʌ́ŋgri 헝그뤼]

hungry     hungry     hungry

**kind**
친절한
[kaind 카인드]

kind    kind    kind    kind

**late**
늦은, 늦게
[leit 레잇]

late    late    late    late

**lonely**
외로운
[lóunlí 로운리]

lonely    lonely    lonely    lonely

**new**
새로운
[njuː 뉴-]

new    new    new    new

**next**
다음의, 다음에
[nekst 넥스트]

next    next    next    next

**nice**
멋진
[nais 나이스]

nice    nice    nice    nice

**only**
오직, 유일한
[óunli 오운리]

only    only    only    only

**round**
둥근, 동그란
[raund 롸운드]

round    round    round

**sad**
슬픈, 슬퍼하는
[sæd 쌔드]

sad    sad    sad    sad    sad

**same**
동일한, 똑같은
[seim 쎄임]

same    same    same    same

**sorry**
죄송한
[sɔ́ːri 써-뤼]

sorry    sorry    sorry    sorry

## (a) 단수와 복수

### These are two helicopters.
[ðiːz ər tuː helikɑːptərs]

이것들은 두 대의 헬리콥터입니다

### These are three blocks.
[ðiːz ər θriː blɑːk]

이것들은 세 개의 블럭입니다

### These are four books.
[ðiːz ər fɔːr buks]

이것들은 네 권의 책입니다

## 문장을 따라 써 보세요

These are two helicopters.

These are two helicopters.

These are three blocks.

These are three blocks.

These are four books.

These are four books.

# These are two teddy bears.
[ði:z ər tu: té di bers]

이것들은 두 개의 곰인형입니다

# These are four toy boats.
[ði:z ər fɔ:r tɔi bouts]

이것들은 네 개의 장난감 보트입니다

# These are three balloons.
[ði:z ər θri: bəlu:ns]

이것들은 세 개의 풍선입니다

These are two teddy bears.

These are two teddy bears.

These are four toy boats.

These are four toy boats.

These are three balloons.

These are three balloons.

- 복수는 명사에 'S'를 붙이며, 'These are~'(이것들은 ~입니다)로 표현하며, 단수는 명사에 'S'를 붙이지 않고, 'This is~(이것은 ~입니다.)로 씁니다.

보기에서 골라 █████ 속에 알맞은 단어를 쓰고 아래 따라 써 봅시다.

보기  four  three  five  two

❶ These are ▨▨▨ helicopters.

이것은 두 대의 헬리콥터이다

These are ____ helicopters.

❷ These are ▨▨ teddy bears.

이것은 두 개의 곰인형이다

These are ____ teddy bears.

❸ These are ▨▨▨

이것은 세 개의 풍선이다

These are ____ balloons.

☆ 다음 그림을 보고 알맞은 단어에 ○표를 하세요.

**4**

## These are three.

이것들은 세 개의 불럭이다

block
blocks

**5**

## These are four toy.

이것들은 네 개의 장난감배이다

boat
boats

**6**

## These are four.

이것들은 네권의 책이다

book
books

## 단어를 따라 써 보세요

### travel
여행, 여행하다

[trǽvəl] 튜뤄블

travel  travel  travel  travel

### trip
여행

[trip] 츄립

trip trip trip trip trip

### ship
배

[ʃip] 쉽

ship  ship  ship  ship  ship

### doll
인형

[dal] 덜

doll  doll  doll  doll

### subway
지하철

[sʌ́bwéi] 써브웨이

subway  subway  subway

## picnic
소풍

picnic    picnic    picnic    picnic

[piknik] 피크닉

## place
장소, 곳

place    place    place    place

[pleis] 플레이스

## helicopter
헬리콥터

helicopter helicopter helicopter

[héliáptər] 헬리콥터

## road
길, 도로

road road road road

[roud] 로우드

## seat
자리, 좌석

seat    seat    seat    seat

[siːt] 씨-잇트

## station
역, 정거장

station    station    station

[stéiʃən] 스패이션

## life
생명, 생활
[laif] 라이프

life life life life life life

## live
살다
[liv] 리브

live live live live live

## people
사람들, 국민
[píːpl] 피-쁠

people people people

## classmate
동급생
[klǽsméit] 클래스메이트

classmate classmate

## grade
학년
[greid] 그레이드

grade grade grade grade

## library
도서관
[láibreri] 라이브러리

library library library library

## address
주소

[ǽdres] 어드레스

address   address   address

## stamp
우표

[stæmp] 스탬프

stamp   stamp   stamp

## letter
편지

[létər] 레러

letter   letter   letter   letter

## club
클럽, 동호회

[klʌb] 클럽

club   club   club   club   club

## team
팀

[tiːm] 팀

team   team   team

## group
무리, 모임, 떼

[gruːp] 그루웁

group   group   group   group

## (b) a ~ · an ~

# This is a book.
[ðis iz ə buk]

이것은 책입니다

# This is an orange.
[ðis iz ə ɔːrindʒ]

이것은 오렌지입니다

# This is a bag.
[ðis iz ə bæg]

이것은 가방입니다

This is a book.  This is a book.

This is a book.  This is a book.

This is an orange.  This is an orange.

This is an orange.  This is an orange.

This is a bag.     This is a bag.

This is a bag.     This is a bag.

# This is an ice-cream.
[ðis iz ən ais-kri:m]
이것은 아이스크림입니다

# This is a desk.
[ðis iz ə desk]
이것은 책상입니다

# This is a chair.
[ðis iz ə tʃer]
이것은 의자입니다

This is an ice-cream.  This is an ice-cream.

This is an ice-cream.  This is an ice-cream.

This is a desk.   This is a desk.

This is a desk.   This is a desk.

This is a chair.   This is a chair.

This is a chair.   This is a chair.

---

'a, an'은 일반명사 앞에 들어가며, 고유명사와 셀 수 없는 명사 앞에는 들어가지 않습니다. 또, a, e, i, o, u로 시작하는 단어가 앞에 올 때는 'an'을, 그 외에는 'a'를 씁니다.

**❶** This is [    ] ice-cream.

이것은 아이스크림이다.

This is     ice-cream.

**❷** This is [   ] desk.

이것은 책상이다

This is          desk.

**❸** This is [   ] chair.

이것은 의자이다

This is          chair.

❹ This is     book.

이것은 책이다

This is      book.

❺ This is     orange.

이것은 오랜지이다

This is      orange.

❻ This is     bag.

이것은 가방이다

This is      bag.

**단어를 따라 써 보세요**

## album
앨범

[ǽlbəm]
앨범

album  album  album

## class
수업, 학급

[klæs] 클래스

class  class  class  class  class

## computer
컴퓨터

[kəmpjúːtər]
컴퓨-러ㄹ

computer computer computer

## crayon
크레용

[kréiən] 크레이언

crayon  crayon  crayon  crayon

## ink
잉크

[iŋk] 잉크

ink  ink  ink  ink

60

## eraser
지우개

[iréisəʒər]
이레이줘ㄹ

eraser eraser eraser

## board
판자, 게시판

[bɔ:rd] 보ㅡ르드

board    board    board    board

## learn
배우다

[lə:rn] 러ㅡ언

learn learn learn learn learn

## lesson
수업

[lésn] 레슨

lesson lesson lesson lesson

## library
도서관

[láibreri] 라이브뢰뤼

library library library library

## paper
종이

[péipər] 페이펄

paper    paper    paper    paper

## pin
핀

[pin] 핀

pin   pin   pin   pin   pin   pin

## school
학교, 수업

[sku:l] 스꾸울

school   school   school

## student
학생

[stjú:dənt] 스튜던트

student   student   student

## study
공부하다

[stʌ́di] 스떠디

study   study   study

## table
테이블

[téibl] 테이블

table   table   table   table

## test
시험, 검사

[test] 테스트

test   test   test   test   test

## camp
캠프

[kæmp] 캠프

camp    camp    camp    camp

## chalk
분필

[tʃɔːk] 쵸크

chalk chalk chalk chalk chalk

## page
페이지, 쪽

[peidʒ] 페이쥐

page    page    page    page

## teacher
선생님

[tiːtʃər] 티-처-

teacher    teacher

## teach
가르치다

[tiːtʃ] 티치

teach    teach    teach    teach

# I like a grape and a pear.
[ái laik ə greip ənd ə per]

나는 포도와 배를 좋아한다

# It is butter and cheese.
[it iz bʌtər ənd tʃːz]

그것은 버터와 치즈이다

# I like a cake and bread.
[ái laik ə keik ənd bred]

나는 케이크와 빵을 좋아한다

I like a grape and a pear.

I like a grape and a pear.

It is butter and cheese.

It is butter and cheese.

I like a cake and bread.

I like a cake and bread.

# It is lemon or melon.
[it iz lemən ɔr melən]

그것은 레몬 또는 메론이다.

# I like tomato or banana.
[ái laik təmeitou ɔrbənænə]

나는 토마토 또는 바나나를 좋아한다.

# Give me juice or cola.
[giv mi: dʒu:s ɔr koulə]

주스 또는 콜라를 주세요.

It is lemon or melon.

It is lemon or melon.

I like tomato or banana.

I like tomato or banana.

Give me juice or cola.

Give me juice or cola.

---

• 'and'는 '~그리고'라는 표현으로, 이것과 저것 모두를 선택할 때 씁니다. 'It is butter and cheese(이것은 버터와 치즈입니다).' 'or'는 '~아니면, ~또는'의 뜻으로, 둘 중 하나를 선택할 때 씁니다.

☆ 보기에서 골라          속에 알맞은 단어를 쓰고 아래 따라 써 봅시다.

❶ It is lemon       melon.

그것은 레몬 또는 메론이다

It is lemon       melon.

❷ It is butter     cheese.

그것은 버터와 치즈이다

It is butter      cheese.

❸ I like tomatoor    banana.

나는 토마토 또는 바나나를 좋아한다

I like tomato    banana.

and    or

❹ Give me juice [ ] cola.

주스 또는 콜라를 주세요

Give me juice    coke.

❺ I like a grape [ ] a pear.

나는 포도와 배를 좋아한다

I like a grape    a pear.

❻ I like a cake [ ] bread.

나는 케이크와 빵을 좋아한다

I like a cake    bread.

단어를 따라 써 보세요

## apple
사과

[ǽpəl] 애쁠

apple　apple　apple　apple

## butter
버터

[bʌ́tər] 버러ㄹ

butter　butter　butter　butter

## breakfast
아침식사

[brékfəst] 브랙풔스트

breakfast　breakfast　breakfast

## bread
빵

[bred] 브레드

bread　bread　bread

## cheese
치즈

[tʃiːz] 취-즈

cheese cheese cheese cheese

## cake
케이크

[keik] 케이크

cake　cake　cake　cake

## coffee
커피

[kɔ́ːfi] 커-퓌

coffee　coffee　coffee　coffee

## cream
크림

[kriːm] 크뤼-임

cream　cream　cream　cream

## dinner
저녁 식사

[dínər] 디널

dinner　dinner　dinner　dinner

## food
음식

[fuːd] 푸-드

food　food　food　food

## hamburger
햄버거

[hǽmbəːrgər]
햄버거

hamburger　hamburger

## banana
바나나

[bənǽnə]
버내너

banana    banana

## corn
옥수수

[kɔːɾn] 콘

corn corn corn corn corn

## cocumber
오이

[kjúːkʌmbəɾ]
큐컴벌

cocumber        cocumber

## fruit
과일

[fruːt] 푸룻

fruit fruit fruit fruit

## grape
포도

[greip] 그뢰입

grape grape grape grape

## pear
배

[pɛəɾ] 페얼

pear pear pear pear pear

## strawberry
딸기
[strɔ́ːbéri] 스프러-베뤼

strawberry strawberry

## tomato
토마토
[təméitou] 터메이토

tomato tomato tomato

## lemon
레몬
[ǽmbjuləns] 레먼

lemon lemon lemon lemon

## melon
메론
[mélən] 메런

melon melon melon melon

## peach
복숭아
[píːtʃ] 피-치

peach peach peach peach

## juice
주스
[dʒuːs] 쥬-스

juice juice juice

# (d) This is ~ · That is ~

## That is a rabbit.
[ðæt iz ə rǽbit]

저것은 토끼입니다

## This is a doll.
[ðis iz ə dɑll]

이것은 인형입니다

## This is a box.
[ðis iz ə bɑːks]

이것은 상자입니다

74

That is a rabbit.  That is a rabbit.

That is a rabbit.  That is a rabbit.

This is a doll.    This is a doll.

This is a doll.    This is a doll.

This is a box.    This is a box.

This is a box.    This is a box.

# This is a dog.
[ðis iz ə dɔːg]

이것은 개입니다

# That is a duck.
[ðæt iz ə dʌk]

저것은 오리입니다

# That is a ball.
[ðæt iz ə bɔːl]

저것은 공입니다

This is a dog.　　This is a dog.

This is a dog.　　This is a dog.

That is a duck.　That is a duck.

That is a duck.　That is a duck.

That is a ball.　　That is a ball.

That is a ball.　　That is a ball.

물건을 가리키며 말할 때, 가까이 있는 것은 This is~
(이것), 멀리 있는 것은 That is~(저것)으로 표현합니다.

보기에서 골라 [          ] 속에 알맞은 단어를 쓰고 아래 따라 써 봅시다.

**❶** [          ] **a rabbit.**

저것은 토끼이다

a rabbit.

**❷** [          ] **a duck.**

저것은 오리이다

a duck.

**❸** [          ] **a doll.**

이것은 인형이다

a doll.

78

❹          a box.

이것은 상자이다

_____

a box.

❺          a dog.

이것은 개이다

_____

a dog.

❻          a ball.

저것은 공이다

_____

a ball.

## 단어를 따라 써 보세요

### animal
동물

[ǽnəməl]
애너멀

animal animal animal animal

### ant
개미

[ænt] 앤트

ant ant ant ant ant ant

### dog
개

[dɔːg] 더-ㄱ

dog dog dog dog

### lion
사자

[láiən]
라이언

lion lion lion lion lion lion

### elephant
코끼리

[éləfənt]
엘러펀트

elephant elephant

### deer
사슴
[diə*r*]
디얼

deer    deer    deer

### cow
젖소
[kau] 카우

cow   cow   cow   cow   cow

### pig
돼지
[pig] 피그

pig pig pig pig pig

### monkey
원숭이
[mʌ́ŋki] 멍키

monkey    monkey

### eagle
독수리
[iːg] 이-글

eagle    eagle    eagle    eagle

### bird
새
[bəː*r*d]
벌드

bird   bird   bird   bird   bird

## duck
오리

[dʌk] 덕

duck　　duck　　duck　　duck

## chicken
닭

[tʃíkən]
치킨

chicken　　chicken　　chicken

## fish
물고기

[fiʃ] 피쉬

fish　　fish　　fish　　fish

## fly
파리

[flai] 플라이

fly　　fly　　fly　　fly　　fly

## fox
여우

[fɑks] 팍스

fox　　fox　　fox　　fox

## hen
암탉

[hen] 헨

hen　　hen　　hen　　hen　　hen

## horse
말

[hɔːrs] 헐스

horse    horse    horse

## rabbit
토끼

[rǽbit] 래빗

rabbit   rabbit   rabbit   rabbit

## sheep
양

[ʃiːp] 쉽

sheep   sheep   sheep   sheep

## tiger
호랑이

[táigər]
타이거

tiger   tiger   tiger   tiger

## wolf
늑대

[wúlf] 울프

wolf   wolf   wolf   wolf   wolf

## zoo
동물원

[zuː] 쥬

zoo   zoo   zoo   zoo

You are a student.

### You are a student.
[jə ər ə stu:dnt]

당신은 학생입니다

I am a girl.

### I am a girl.
[á ǽm ə gːrl]

나는 소녀입니다

I am happy.

### I am happy.
[á ǽm hǽpi]

나는 행복합니다

You are a student.

You are a student.

I am a girl.          I am a girl.

I am a girl.          I am a girl.

I am happy.          I am happy.

I am happy.          I am happy.

**You are beautiful.**
[jə ər bjuːtifl]

당신은 아름답습니다

**I am a baseball player.**
[á æm ə beisbɔːl plerər]

나는 야구선수입니다

**You are tall.**
[jə ər tɔːl]

당신은 키가 큽니다

You are a beautiful.

You are a beautiful.

I am a baseball player.

I am a baseball player.

You are tall.        You are tall.

You are tall.        You are tall.

'나는'이라고 할 때 'I'를 쓰며, 이때 '~입니다'의 표현에는 'am'을 사용합니다.
'너는'이라고 할 때는 'You'를 쓰며, 이때 '~입니다'의 표현에는 'are'를 사용합니다.

⭐ 보기에서 골라 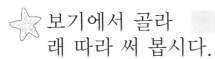 속에 알맞은 단어를 쓰고 아래 따라 써 봅시다.

❶ _____ a girl.

나는 소녀이다

_____

a girl.

❷ _____ beautiful.

당신은 아름답다

_____

beautiful.

❸ _____ a baseball player.

나는 야구선수이다.

_____

a baseball player.

보기     I am     You are

**4**          a student.

너는 학생이다

_____

a student.

---

**5**         tall.

당신은 키가 크다.

_____

tall.

---

**6**         happy.

나는 행복하다

_____

happy.

단어를 따라 써 보세요

## friend
친구

[frend] 프렌

friend  friend  friend

## girl
소녀

[gə:rl] 거얼

girl  girl  girl  girl

## he
그는, 그가

[hi:] 히-

he  he  he  he  he  he

## hers
그녀의 것

[hə:rz] 허어즈

hers  hers  hers

## beautiful
아름다운

[bju:təfəl] 뷰-러풀

beautiful  beautiful  beautiful

## foolish
어리석은
[fúːliʃ] 푸-울리쉬

foolish foolish foolish foolish

## lady
숙녀, 부인
[léidi] 레이디

lady lady lady lady lady

## good
좋은, 착한
[gud] 굿

good good good good

## free
자유로운
[friː] 프뤼-

free free free free free

## hungry
배고픈
[hʌ́ŋgri] 헝그뤼

hungry hungry hungry

## aunt
아주머니, 이모
[ænt] 앤트

aunt aunt aunt aunt

## she
그녀는, 그녀가

[ʃiː] 쉬

she she she she she

## kind
친절한

[kaind] 카인드

kind kind kind kind kind

## lonely
외로운

[lóunli] 외로운

lonely lonely lonely lonely

## nice
멋진

[nais] 나이스

nice nice nice nice nice

## poor
가난한, 불쌍한

[puər] 포올

poor poor poor poor

## child
어린이

[tʃaild] 촤일드

child child child child

## quiet
조용한
[kwaiət] 콰이어트

quiet    quiet    quiet    quiet

## sick
아픈, 병든
[sik] 씩

sick   sick   sick   sick   sick

## you
너, 당신
[ju:] 유

you   you   you   you

## yours
너의 것
[juərz] 유얼스

yours   yours   yours

## baby
아기
[béibi] 베이비

baby   baby   baby   baby

## stupid
어리석은
[stju:pid] 스투피드

stupid   stupid   stupid   stupid

# He is my father.
[hiː iz mai fɑːðər]

그는 나의 아버지입니다

# She is a model.
[ʃi iz ər mɑːdl]

그녀는 모델입니다

# She is a nurse.
[ʃi iz ər nːrs]

그녀는 간호사입니다

# 문장을 따라 써 보세요

He is my father.    He is my father.

He is my father.    He is my father.

She is a model. She is a model.

She is a model. She is a model.

She is a nurse.  She is a nurse.

She is a nurse.  She is a nurse.

# He is a cook.
[hiː iz ə kuk]

그는 요리사입니다

# She is a scientist.
[ʃi iz ə saiəntist]

그녀는 과학자입니다

# She is a teacher.
[ʃi iz ə tiːtʃər]

그녀는 선생님입니다

He is a cook.    He is a cook.

He is a cook.    He is a cook.

She is a scientist.  She is a scientist.

She is a scientist.  She is a scientist.

She is a teacher.  She is a teacher.

She is a teacher.  She is a teacher.

- 남자를 가리킬 때는 'He is~'로 표현하고
- 여자를 가리킬 때는 'She is~'로 표현합니다.

보기에서 골라 　　　　 속에 알맞은 단어를 쓰고 아
래 따라 써 봅시다.

❶ 　　　　　　 a teacher.

그녀는 선생님이다

_____

a teacher.

❷ 　　　　　 a nurse.

그녀는 간호사이다

_____

a nurse.

❸ 　　　　　　 my father.

그는 나의 아버지이다.

_____

my father.

**4**　　　　　a cook.

그는 요리사이다.

_____

a cook.

**5**　　　a scientist.

그녀는 과학자이다.

_____

a scientist.

**6**　　　　　a model.

그녀는 조종사이다.

_____

a model.

단어를 따라 써 보세요

## model
모델

[mɔ́dl] 모들

model model model model

## cook
요리사

[kúk] 쿡

cook cook cook cook cook

## doctor
의사

[dáktər] 닥터 ㄹ

doctor doctor doctor

## job
일, 직업

[dʒab] 좝

job job job job job

## singer
가수

[síŋər] 싱어-

singer singer singer singer

## nurse
간호사

[nəːrs] 널쓰

nurse nurse nurse

## pilot
조종사

[páilət] 파일럿

pilot pilot pilot pilot pilot

## police
경찰

[pəlíːs] 펄리-스

police police police police

## scientist
과학자

[sáiəntist] 사이언티스트

scientist scientist

## soldier
군인

[sóuldʒər] 소울저-

soldier soldier soldier soldier

## farmer
농부

[fáːrmər] 파-머-

farmer farmer farmer farmer

**stewardess**
스튜어디스

[stjúːərdis] 스튜어-디스

stewardess    stewardess

**fisherman**
어부

[fiʃərmən] 피셔-먼

fisherman fisherman fisherman

**lead**
인도하다

[líd] 리드

lead    lead    lead    lead    lead

**writer**
작가

[ráitər] 롸이터-

writer    write    write    write

**life**
생명, 생활

[láif] 라이프

life    life    life    life    life

**live**
살다

[liv] 리브

live    live    live    live    live

## talent
탤런트

[tǽlələnt]
탤런트

talent     talent     talent     talent

## judge
판사

[dʒʌ́dʒ] 져지

judge     judge     judge     judge

## artist
화가

[ά:rtist]
아-티스트

artist     artist     artist     artist

## party
파티, 모임

[pά:rti] 파-르티

party     party     party

## lady
숙녀, 부인

[léídi] 레이디

lady     lady     lady

# What is this?
[wɑːt iz ðis]

이것은 무엇입니까?

# It is the river.

➡ It's the river.
[its ðəː rivər]

이것은 강입니다

# It is the air.

➡ It's the air.
[its ðiː er]

이것은 공기입니다

What is this?        What is this?

What is this?        What is this?

It's the river.        It's the river.

It's the river.        It's the river.

It's the air. It's the air. It's the air.

It's the air. It's the air. It's the air.

## What is this?
[wɑːt iz ðis]

이것은 무엇입니까?

## It is the sea.

➡ ## It's the sea.
[its ðəː siː]

이것은 바다입니다

## It is the moon.

➡ ## It's the moon.
[its ðəː muːn]

이것은 달입니다

What is this?　　What is this?

What is this?　　What is this?

It is the sea.　　It is the sea.

It is the sea.　　It is the sea.

It is the moon.　　It is the moon.

It is the moon.　　It is the moon.

• It is는 It's로 쓸 수 있습니다. 이렇게 줄여 쓰는 것을 단축형이라고 합니다. 그 밖의 be 동사가 들어가 문장이 단축된 형은 다음처럼 더 있습니다.

- They are = They're
- We are = We're
- What is = What's
- How is = How's

- You are = You're
- I am = I'm
- She is = She's
- He is = He's

보기와 같이 ▨▨▨▨▨ 속에 알맞은 단어를 쓰고 아래 따라 써 봅시다.

**보기**   It is  the moon ➡ It's  the moon

**❶** It is  the mountain.
　　　 the mountain.

이것은 산이다

_____

the mountain.

**❷** It is  the island.
　　　 the island.

이것은 섬이다

_____

the island.

**❸** It is  the lake.
　　　 the lake.

이것은 호수이다

_____

the lake.

**❹** It is the air.
　　　　　the air.

이것은 공기이다

_____

_____
the air.

**❺** It is the river.
　　　　　the river.

이것은 강이다

_____

_____
the river.

**❻** It is the sea.
　　　　　the sea.

이것은 바다이다

_____

_____
the sea.

**❼** It is the moon.
　　　　　the moon.

이것은 달이다

_____

_____
the cloud.

단어를 따라 써 보세요

## apartment
아파트

[əpάːrtmənt]
아파-아트먼트

apartment     apartment

## balcony
베란다

[bǽlkrni] 밸커니

balcony   balcony   balcony

## bed
침대

[bed] 뱃

bed   bed   bed   bed

## bell
종, 초인종

[bel] 벨

bell   bell   bell   bell   bell   bell

## bench
긴 의자, 벤취

[bentʃ] 벤취

bench   bench   bench   bench

## chair
의자

[tʃɛ́ər] 췌얼

chair chair chair chair

## curtain
커튼

[kə́:rtn] 커튼

curtain curtain curtain curtain

## door
문

[dɔ:r] 도얼

door door door door

## elevator
엘리베이터

[éləvéitər] 엘리베이터

elevagtor elevagtor elevagtor

## garden
정원

[gá:rdn] 가ー든

garden garden garden garden

## gas
가스

[gæs] 개스

gas gas gas gas gas gas

## home
집

[hóum] 홈

home home home

## house
집

[haus] 하우스

house house house house

## kitchen
부엌

[kítʃin] 킷췬

kitchen kitchen

## knife
칼

[naif] 나이프

knife knife knife knife

## lobby
로비(현관의 홀)

[lábi] 라비

lobby lobby lobby lobby

## mailbox
우편함

[méilbáks] 메일박스

mailbox mailbox mailbox

**mirror**
거울

[mírər] 미뤄-ㄹ

mirror   mirror   mirror   mirror

**radio**
라디오

[réidiou] 뢰이디오

radio   radio   radio   radio

**roof**
지붕

[ruːf] 루-프

roof   roof   roof   roof   roof

**room**
방

[ruːm] 루-움

room   room   room   room

**sofa**
소파

[soufə] 쏘우풔

sofa   sofa   sofa

**window**
창(창문)

[wíndou] 윈도우

window   window   window

**단어를 따라 써 보세요**

### afraid
무서워하여

[əfréid어프뤠이드]

afraid   afraid   afraid   afraid

### busy
바쁜

[bízì 비지]

busy   busy   busy   busy

### careful
조심스러운

[kɛərfəl 캐얼풀]

careful   careful   careful

### empty
텅 빈

[émpti 엠티]

empty   empty   empty   empty

### enough
충분한

[inʌ́f 이너프]

enough   enough   enough

| **every**<br>모든<br>[évriː 에브뤼] | every every every every |
| **fair**<br>공평한, 공정한<br>[fɛər 페얼] | fair fair fair fair fair |
| **few**<br>거의 없는<br>[fjuː 퓨-] | few few few few few |
| **foolish**<br>어리석은<br>[fúːliʃ 푸-울리쉬] | foolish foolish foolish foolish |
| **fresh**<br>새로운, 신선한<br>[freʃ 프뤳쉬] | fresh fresh fresh |
| **ill**<br>아픈, 병든<br>[il 일] | ill ill ill ill ill ill |

## 자음 발음 기호

[p] 프   [b] 브   [t] 트   [d] 드   [k] 크

[g] 그   [m] 므   [n] 느   [ŋ] 응   [l] 르

[f] 프   [v] 브   [θ] 쓰   [ð] 드   [s] 스

[z] 즈   [ʃ] 쉬   [ʒ] 쥐   [tʃ] 취   [dʒ] 쥐

[r] 르   [h] 흐   [j] 이   [w] 우

## 모음 발음 기호

[a]
아

[i]
이

[e]
에

[æ]
애

[ɔ]
어/오

[u]
우

[ʌ]
어

[ə]
어

[iː]
이-

[aː]
아-

[ɔː]
오-

[uː]
우-

[au]
아우

[ei]
에이

[ou]
오우

[ai]
아이

[ɔi]
오이

[əːr]
어-ㄹ

[iːr]
이-ㄹ

[iər]
이어ㄹ

[uər]
우어-ㄹ

## 자음 발음 기호

### [p] 프

**pen** [pen] [펜] 펜

아랫입술과 윗입술을 붙였다 떼면서 숨을 급히 내쉬듯이 강하게 우리말의 [ㅍ]하고 같은 소리를 내세요.

### [b] 브

**blue** [bluː][블루] 파랑

아랫입술과 윗입술을 붙였다 떼면서 우리 말의 [ㅂ]에 가까운 소리를 내어 보세요.

### [d] 드

**desk** [desk][데스ㅋ]책상

윗니와 아랫니 사이에 혀를 약간 대고 우리 말의 [ㄷ]에 가까운 소리로 발음하세요.

### [t] 트

**tree**[triː] [트리]나무

혀끝을 윗니 뒤에 살짝 붙여서 우리말의 [ㅌ]에 가까운 소리로 발음해 보세요.

### [f] 프

**fox** [faks] [파ㄱ쓰]여우

아랫입술을 윗니에 살짝 붙이고 그 사이로 우리말의 [프]와 같이 소리를 내세요.

### [k] 크

**kid** [kid] [키드] 아이

윗니와 아랫니를 약간만 벌리고 혀의 뒷부분을 살짝 들어 우리말의 [ㅋ]과 가까운 소리로 발음하세요.

## [l] 르

**lemon**[lémən][레몬]레몬

아랫입술과 윗입술을 붙였다 떼면서 숨을 급히 내쉬듯이 강하게 우리말의 [ㅍ]하고 같은 소리를 내세요.

## [g] 그

**grape**[greip][그레이프]포도

윗니와 아랫니를 붙이고 혀의 뒷부분을 살짝 들고 우리말의 [ㄱ]과 가까운 소리로 발음하세요.

## [ŋ] 응

**pink**[piŋk][핑크]분홍색

혀의 뒷부분을 입천장 뒤에 살짝 대면서 콧소리로 [응]하고 소리를 내세요.

## [m] 므

**monkey**[mʌ́ŋki][몽키]원숭이

입술을 붙였다 떼면서 콧소리 우리말 [ㅁ]에 가까운 소리를 내세요.

## [n] 느

**nurse**[nəːrs][너얼스]간호사

혀끝을 윗니 뒤에 살짝 대었다 떼면서 콧소리로 우리말의 [ㄴ]에 가까운 소리를 내세요.

## [v] 브

**vacation** [veikéiʃən][붸-케이션]방학

윗니를 아랫입술에 가볍게 대고 우리말의 [ㅂ]에 가까운 소리로 발음해 보세요.

## [s] 스

**sky**[skai][스카이]하늘

윗니와 아랫니를 붙인 사이로 바람을 내보내듯 [스으]하고 소리를 내세요.

## [ʒ] 쥐

**age**[eidʒ][에이쥐]나이

입술을 동그랗게 하고 바람을 내보내듯 [쥐]하고 발음을 해 보세요.

## [z] 즈

**zebra**[zibrə][쥐브라]얼룩말

입술을 양옆으로 살짝 당기고, 윗니와 아랫니를 붙인 사이로 바람을 내보내듯 [즈]소리를 내세요.

## [θ] 쓰

**thin** [θin] [씬] 얇은

윗니와 아랫니 사이로 혀끝을 약간 내밀며 [쓰]하고 소리를 내세요.

## [ʃ] 쉬

**shop** [ʃɑp] [샵] 상점

입술을 동그랗게 하고 바람을 내보내듯 [쉬]하고 발음을 해 보세요.

## [ð] 드

**that** [ðæt] [댓] 저것

윗니와 아랫니 사이로 혀끝을 약간 내밀며 [드]하고 소리를 내세요.

# [tʃ] 취

**chicken**[tʃíkin][취킨]닭

입술을 동그랗게 말아 내밀고 [취]하고 발음해 보세요.

# [dʒ] 쥐

**juice**[dʒuːs][쥬-스]주스

입술을 동그랗게 말아서 숨을 내뱉듯 [쥐]하고 발음해 보세요.

# [r] ㄹ

**ruler**[rúːlər][룰러]자

혀끝을 살짝 말아 올리면서 우리말의 [ㄹ]을 발음해 보세요.

# [h] ㅎ

**hat** [hæt] [햇]모자

윗니와 아랫니 사이로 바람을 불어내듯이 [흐]하고 힘있게 발음해 보세요.

# [j] 이

**yellow**[jélou][옐로-우]노랑

우리말 [이]에서 [야]로 자연스럽게 넘어가듯 발음해 보세요.

# [w] 우

**watch**[watʃ][왓치]손목시계

입술을 동그랗게 오므리고 [우]하고 소리를 내세요.

## 모음 발음 기호

### [a] 아

shop [ʃɑp] [샵]가게

입을 크게 벌려 입 안쪽에서 [아]하고 소리를 내세요.

### [i] 이

ship [ʃip] [쉽] 배

[이]하고 짧게 발음하세요.

### [iː] 이-

bee [biː] [비-] 벌

우리 말의 [이]를 길게 끄는 소리와 같이 발음하세요.

### [e] 에

egg [eg] [에그]달걀

입을 약간 벌리고 우리 말의 [에]에 가까운 발음으로 소리 내세요.

### [æ] 에

apple[æpl][애플]사과

입을 약간 벌리고 우리 말의 [애]와 같은 발음으로 강하게 발음하세요.

### [ɑː] 아-

arm[ɑːrm][아-암]팔

우리 말의 [아]를 길게 끄는 소리와 같이 발음하세요.

[ɔ] 오

**soil** [sɔil] [소일] 흙

우리 말의 [오]보다 입을 크게 벌리고, 입 안쪽에서 [오]하고 발음해 보세요.

[ɔː] 오-

**water** [wɔ́ːtər] [워럴]물

입 안쪽에서 [오]하고 길게 발음해 보세요.

[u] 우

**cookie** [kúki] [쿠키]쿠키

우리말의 [우]에 가까운 소리이지만 입술을 좀더 좁게 오므리고 발음하세요.

[ʌ] 어

**umbrella** [mbrélə][엄브렐러]우산

우리 말의 [아]와 [어]의 중간 소리로 입을 약간 더 벌리고 [어]에 가깝게 발음하세요.

[ə] 어

**lion** [láiən][라이언]사자

입을 약간 벌리고 혀를 아랫니 뒤에 대고 짧고 약하게 [어]하고 소리를 내세요.

[ai] 아이

**kite** [kait][카이트]연

입을 크게 벌리고 [아]를 강하게 발음하면서 [이]를 약하게 소리 내세요.

## [au] 아우

house[haus][하우스]집

[아]를 강하게 발음하고 이어서 [우]를 약하게 소리 내세요.

## [ei] 에이

train[trein][트레인]열차

[에]를 강하게 발음하고 이어서 [이]를 약하게 소리 내세요.

## [ou] 오우

roa [roud][로드]길

[오]를 강하게 발음하고 이어서 [우]를 약하게 소리 내세요.

## [ɔi] 오이

toy [tɔi][토이]장난감

[오]와 [이]를 연이어서 소리를 내세요.

## [ɛər] 에어르

airplane[ɛərplèin]
[에어르플레인]비행기

[에]를 강하게 발음하고 이 이서 [어르]를 약하게 소리 내세요.

## [uər] 우어르

tour[tuər][투어리] 여행

[우]를 강하게 발음하고 이어서 [어르]를 약하게 소리 내세요.

[iɚr] 이어ㄹ

year[iɚr][이어ㄹ]해, 1년

[이]를 강하게 발음하고 이어서 [어ㄹ]를 약하게 소리 내세요.

[ɔːɚr] 오어ㄹ

store[stɔːɚr][스토어ㄹ]가게

[오]를 강하게 발음하고 이어서 [어ㄹ]를 약하게 소리 내세요.

① bear      ② table

③ computer.   ④ banana.

⑤ bag      ⑥ Sung-won

① That    ② I

③ We    ④ He

⑤ This    ⑥ This

① am    ② go

③ play    ④ are

⑤ is    ⑥ is

① smart    ② young

③ happy    ④ beautifu

⑤ ugly    ⑥ smart

① two    ② two

③ three    ④ blocks

⑤ boats    ⑥ books

① an    ② a

③ a    ④ a

⑤ an    ⑥ a

① or    ② and

③ or    ④ or

⑤ and    ⑥ and

① That is    ② That is

③ This is    ④ This is

⑤ This is    ⑥ That is

p.88p  I am    You are

① I am      ② You are
③ I am      ④ You are
⑤ You are   ⑥ I am

p.98p   He is~  She is~

① She is    ② She is
③ He is     ④ He is
⑤ She is    ⑥ She is

p.108p  It is~ → It's~ I am~ → I'm~

① It's  the mountain.

② It's  the island.

③ It's the lake.

④ It's the air.

⑤ It's the river.

⑥ It's the sea.

⑦ It's the moom

초등 영어문장 규칙 배우기(1)
# 기초문장 · 단어 따라쓰기

**초판 1쇄 발행** 2016년 2월 10일

**글** Y&M 어학 연구소

**펴낸이** 서영희 | **펴낸곳** 와이 앤 엠

**편집** 임명아 | **책임교정** 하연정

**본문인쇄** 명성 인쇄 | **제책** 정화 제책

**제작** 이윤식 | **마케팅** 강성태

**주소** 03659 서울특별시 서대문구 명지2길 21, 102호

**전화** (02)308-3891 | Fax (02)308-3892

E-mail yam3891@naver.com

**등록** 2007년 8월 29일 제312-2007-00004호

ISBN 978-89-93557-68-8    63740

본사는 출판물 윤리강령을 준수합니다.